DEVELOPING STUDENT SUPPORT GROUPS

A Tutor's Guide

DEVELOPING STUDENT SUPPORT GROUPS

A Tutor's Guide

ROSIE BINGHAM

and

JAQUIE DANIELS

Gower

Published by
Gower Publishing Limited
Gower House
Croft Road
Aldershot
Hampshire GU11 3HR
England

Gower
Old Post Road
Brookfield
Vermont 05036
USA

British Library Cataloguing in Publication Data
Bingham, Rosie
Developing student support groups : a tutor's guide
1. Peer counselling of students 2. College students – Services for 3. Student assistance programs
I. Title II. Daniels, Jaquie
378.1`9`4

ISBN 0 566 08117 2

Printed and bound in Great Britain by MPG Books Ltd, Bodmin, Cornwall

CONTENTS

1	**Introduction**	1
1.1	Who is this guide for?	2
1.2	What are student support groups?	2
1.3	What is the purpose of student support groups?	6
1.4	What is the role of the tutor?	8
1.5	What is the role of the student?	11
1.6	Summary	13
2	**Advance Planning - Setting Up**	15
2.1	How will the student support groups be structured?	16
2.2	What will the student support groups be doing?	24
2.3	What structured support materials could be useful?	28
2.4	What could you do at the first session?	31
2.5	Summary	35
3	**Advance Planning - Monitoring, Support and Review**	37
3.1	Why do you want to monitor and support the student support groups?	38
3.2	How will you organise the monitoring and support process?	44
3.3	What will you monitor and review?	50
3.4	What methods will you use to review?	51
3.5	Summary	55
4	**Advance Planning - Assessment**	57
4.1	Will you use assessment with support groups?	58
4.2	What will you assess?	58
4.3	Who will assess?	59
4.4	How will marks be allocated?	65
4.5	What evidence can be provided?	67
4.6	Summary	73
5	**Dealing with Potential Difficulties**	75
5.1	What are the potential difficulties in working with student support groups?	76
5.2	What are some of the strategies needed to overcome potential difficulties?	77
5.3	Summary	80
6	**Conclusion**	83
7	**References**	87

INTRODUCTION

1.1 Who is this guide for?
1.2 What are student support groups?
1.3 What is the purpose of student support groups?
1.4 What is the role of the tutor?
1.5 What is the role of the student?
1.6 Summary

This practical guide aims to offer information and ideas to help you set up and maintain student support groups. It draws on a range of practice which may also help you develop your current strategies further and offers suggestions to enable your students to form learning support or social groups more quickly. The guide has been written in an interactive format, with self-completion boxes for you to fill in, should you wish to do so.

The information in this guide is based on Sheffield Hallam University tutors' experiences of working with support groups, from secondary sources and from data given by other Further and Higher Education providers. We are grateful for the time and effort provided by all the contributors.

The support groups studied covered the full range of disciplines and were purposefully set up by tutors, some working as individuals, others in course teams in both traditional and open learning settings. Common features included aiming to develop students' academic, personal and professional skills, increasing student autonomy and formalising peer support for the learning process. The tutor groups included both traditional and non-traditional students, with course numbers ranging from 10 to 360. Many involved assessment. Approaches to setting up and working with the support groups varied, and the strategies used are included in the guide.

This introduction covers the following questions:

- **Who is this guide for?**

- **What are student support groups?**

- **What is the purpose of student support groups?**

- **What is the role of the tutor?**

- **What is the role of the student?**

1.1 WHO IS THIS GUIDE FOR?

Further and Higher Education have recently undergone a period of rapid change, with increasing numbers, changing markets and ever-reducing resources. There is an increasing demand for all students to be offered more flexible provision, with a greater emphasis towards more open and distance learning. These changes have had an impact on the role of the tutor who is required to cover the same amount of material in less contact time, as well as fostering the personal and professional development of individual students. The emphasis on encouraging more autonomous and independent learners, along with the developments in open learning and assessment, may leave many students feeling isolated and unsupported in their learning experience.

Student support groups are increasingly being used to address some of these changes, whether in traditional-contact courses or in distance learning provision.

This guide is for members of staff who are:

- **already working with student support groups**
- **working with learners on open or distance learning programmes**
- **considering initiating or developing work with student support groups**
- **thinking of ways of supporting learners more through a group work structure**
- **aiming to encourage student peer support.**

Peer support can be channelled and developed to increase support for learners and to help tutors deal with the increased demands on their time. However, establishing and developing student support groups does require careful planning, support and co-ordination from tutors, particularly in the initial stages of implementation. **Without this investment of time for early and effective planning and preparation, student support groups will not be successful.**

1.2 WHAT ARE STUDENT SUPPORT GROUPS?

You may already be working with some form of student support group, which may come under the name of:

• **task group**	• **work group**	• **peer group**
• **learning group**	• **set**	• **support group**
• **learning set**	• **study group**	
• **tutorial group**	• **social group**	

There are two main models of student or peer support:

1.2.1 The mentoring model

Students in later years of a programme support those who are at the beginning of a programme. The relationship is usually one-to-one, though it can also often be found within a group setting. Some schemes are now looking to offer academic credit to the mentors, in recognition of the value of the learning experienced by both mentor and mentees.

1.2.2 The self-supporting group model

The self-supporting group usually comprises students from the same year. The group may work together over a period of time to support each other in a variety of ways, including academically, socially, professionally and/or emotionally. This book concentrates on this particular model of peer support.

Many students attending full-time courses create informal peer support groups for themselves at some time during their studies. The speed at which this happens will depend on, for example, the tutor's role, the level of group work within the classroom and individual needs. This, to some extent, will leave peer support to chance and may not involve all learners on a programme or unit. Those students following more open or distance learning or part-time courses/programmes may find peer-group support even more left to chance.

On a more structured basis, students may be expected by tutors to form support groups on a unit, programme or course-wide basis. The group could be determined by either the tutor, or the students themselves and may be required to work together over a period of time on individual or group based tasks or assignments. The group may facilitate team working and also offer some form of personal and/or social support/development. The level of peer support will be determined by the defined aims or purpose of the group, its functions and the input and support of the tutor. The purpose and function of the group will define the depth and type of support which students are able to give each other.

1.2.3 What are the potential benefits?

Students who have experienced being members of support groups identified the following benefits:

'Through my experiences, I regard the learner support groups as a vital and integral part of coursework at this level of learning.'

'It is a good way of ironing out any problems which may occur. 'Two or more heads' are always better than one. It worked very well. I could get together with others and discuss the course work and develop my skills and attitude further than working alone.'

'Very helpful. Takes some of the pressure off.'

'Useful way of exchanging ideas, enjoyable way of sharing researched material.'

'Confidence about myself around others and speaking about my ideas.'

'Made me feel valued.'

'Useful way of learning how to allocate tasks.'

'Helped revision, built on knowledge of other people with a wider knowledge base.'

'Improved my abilities in being part of a team.'

The following benefits were identified in response to the question 'If you hadn't been part of a support group in the last semester, what difference do you think that would have made to you?

'I would not have understood the topic as well as I did.'

'Would have felt more isolated.'

'It would have been more difficult for me to evaluate how well I was performing with respect to coursework and express openly any concerns I have had.'

'Fairly difficult. Higher education is a bit daunting at the start, but with being part of a support group, and supporting and encouraging one another, it helped me enormously.'

'The support group helped all members in developing assignments and general moral support. I would have been very worried about my academic abilities in higher education without the encouragement and reassurance I received from the support group.'

Student support groups can:

- **be part of a process through which students can learn to become more self-directed**
- **put the most positive aspects of self-directed or autonomous learning into practice.**

If student support groups are set up in the initial stages of the learning experience, at whatever level, then it is more likely that students:

- **will settle down more quickly into the programme**

- **will be more likely to be satisfied with their experience and less likely to drop out**

- **will be better able to cope with the education system**

- **will benefit socially, academically and professionally from the interaction with their peers**

- **will feel less isolated**

1.2.4 What are the possible issues?

The scenario listed above may sound idyllic! In practice, however, there may be occasions when learner support groups do not live up to these expectations. This may be particularly so when the learners themselves are not supported by the tutor and when aims are not clear.

At this stage, you might find it helpful to identify and keep a note of some of the possible issues for you and your learners.

This guide may help address some of these issues, in particular through the discussion on the process of planning for learner support groups. You might find it useful to refer back to these issues after you have worked through it (see also Chapter 4).

1.3 WHAT IS THE PURPOSE OF STUDENT SUPPORT GROUPS?

1.3.1 Broad aims

Student support groups can have several very broad aims. These will define the purpose of the student support group and help you to work out the structure that most suits you and your teaching/learning situation. Aims can be combined and may often overlap and develop once the groups have been established. A support group may only gradually become a resource for personal and emotional support, for example.

It is important to be clear about the aims or purpose of the student support group from the outset to ensure its effectiveness. You might also consider how these relate to the intended learning outcomes.

Please tick the broad aims of a support group which you consider relevant to your own teaching/learning situation. There are also spaces in which to add your own ideas.	
to act as a resource for **understanding common issues** related directly to the learning situation *e.g. the new environment, course information*	☐
to support the development of **subject related knowledge and understanding** through sharing information and ideas	☐
to support the development of **study skills** *e.g. research skills, academic writing, critical/analytical skills*	☐
to support the development of **interpersonal skills** *e.g. effective communication, team building*	☐
to support **personal and professional development**	☐
to act as a resource for **personal and emotional support**	☐
to encourage **co-operation**	☐
to increase **motivation**	☐
to increase the **level of support** available for students	☐

1.3.2 Activities and Learning Outcomes

The aims and purpose of the support group also need to be clearly set out and defined for the students. These can be re-enforced by the Learning Outcomes and course activities designed to meet them. The following table provides examples of how the activities and tasks of the support group could achieve the aims previously listed, along with suggested learning outcomes taken from course descriptions across different subject areas. Thus, the student support group work is not only often relevant to the aims and learning outcomes of a course or programme, but can act as a vehicle through which these can be achieved. The work done in student support groups does not have to be completely separate from it. This list is by no means exhaustive and has not included specific subject issues. There is space for your own ideas.

Please look through the table and select and add your own ideas, as appropriate.	
Activities/Tasks	**Example of Learning Outcomes**
Share experiences, skills and knowledge; group tasks or projects; share ideas on assignments.	Work effectively in a team to solve problems and make decisions in a business context. *(Computing Management Science)*
Support on placement or work experience. Research and share different aspects of course information and/or the environment.	Develop group working skills during block week and practical sessions. *(Urban and Regional Studies)*
Develop awareness of own and other learning styles, share work in progress, work through skills packs.	Analyse and monitor their personal learning style. *(Leisure and Food Management)*
Reflect on the learning process in order to identify individual strengths, areas to develop further and how to achieve this.	Understand their own strengths and weaknesses and developing strategies to deal with them. *(Cultural Studies)*
Give and receive positive and constructive feedback, share contacts. Peer assessment.	Engage in the initial review of their own work and that of other students. *(Cultural Studies)*
Report on individual and group progress in the appropriate forum (e.g. group tutorials), complete activities related to team work and effective group work. Peer assessment and feedback.	Evaluate individual and team performance through peer assessment, diaries and review. *(Science)*
Support each group member in developing his/her own learning outcomes for the course and in finding ways of achieving these learning outcomes. Self-assessment.	Provide a rationale for mentorship. *(Education)*

Activities/Tasks	Example of Learning Outcomes

1.4 WHAT IS THE ROLE OF THE TUTOR?

Methods of learning and teaching have had to adapt to new expectations and have had a marked effect on the traditional role of the tutor, which is moving from delivering knowledge to facilitating the learning process.

It is helpful to consider this different and often broader role of the tutor as it has implications for developing and working with student support groups. Student support groups will need the support of their tutor and this role will differ according to how the aims and purpose of the student support group are defined. Whatever the input, the tutor plays a vital part in the effectiveness of student support groups.

For those working in a more traditional setting, the tutor's role in the classroom and the group work activities offered, can have a significant effect on how soon both formal and informal peer support groups are formed and how effective they are. Using group work in the classroom means that students will know each others' names and use the coffee breaks effectively to support each other in their learning.

For those tutors working with open and distance learners, it is vital that you demonstrate your recognition of the value of support group work and the help it can offer more isolated learners. Adopting appropriate activities within tasks, whether during residentials, monthly meetings or at a distance, becomes a highly significant element in the effectiveness of the support group. With this recognition in mind, whatever activities you choose for your learners will contribute to the framework in which they will work most effectively.

1.4.1 Supporting learners in developing student support groups

The role of the tutor can be placed along a continuum according to the degree of structure or direction they provide. Whatever approach is taken, the tutor will always have a positive role in the forming of student support groups. The more structure is provided by the tutor, the more direct this role is, and the more to the left of the continuum (below) it will be.

tutor structured

e.g. Lecture
Presentation

student structured

e.g. Student
presentation
Student structured
support group meeting

Initially, at the beginning of a course, you may start off on the left of the continuum using a more formal, structured approach and then gradually adopt more of an observer or monitoring role, encouraging students towards more autonomous decision making. In this case, you will move more towards the right of the continuum.

To encourage the most effective or productive learning context, it is useful to be clear about your own role and plan your approach in advance. Your support is needed by your students throughout, but the nature of the support may change as the student support groups develop. You may find it helpful to plan this with other tutors to share ideas, approaches and resources, thereby forming your own support group.

You might find it useful to consider how far you are already working with students to support them in their being able to manage their own learning and to form support groups. The table below provides some ideas of how a tutor might support students to become autonomous and to support each other. Priorities will be determined by the defined purpose of the student support groups. Some of the ideas identified may be more relevant at the initial stages of support group development, such as promoting a culture of co-operation, and others, at the latter stages, such as encouraging risk-taking.

Please tick the appropriate column in the table. There are spaces for your own ideas on your role

The columns are coded as follows:

1 = *this role is new to me/is irrelevant*   3 = *I feel adequate in this area*
2 = *I need more practice*   4 = *I feel confident about this*

The role of the tutor	1	2	3	4
Designing structured learning materials to support students				
Providing clear aims and structure to initial support group activities				
Negotiating goals with students				
Providing opportunities for students to evaluate their own learning				
Reviewing and monitoring progress regularly with students				
Encouraging students to help each other to aid learning and development				
Designing assessment strategies for the group				
Providing opportunities for students to assess themselves				
Promoting a culture of co-operation				
Sharing ideas and resources with other tutors				
Encouraging learners to solve problems				
Acting as a resource/facilitator for students				
Giving prompt and constructive feedback				
Encouraging risk-taking				
Managing and making effective use of available time				
Identifying activities to match students' different learning styles				

You may see your role in working with support groups as being different from that of working with your tutor group. Clarifying your role at the outset provides a clear structure for working and avoids conflict created by unrealistic expectations.

You might find it helpful to share and discuss your ideas with a colleague. You might also consider asking your students to outline their own expectations of you. You could then compare this to your own list and make additions as appropriate.

1.5 WHAT IS THE ROLE OF THE STUDENT?

The tutor role changes as (s)he moves along the continuum, as will the role of the students. It is helpful to think about what this change will require of students and to prepare them to manage it successfully. There may be some particular student-related issues to consider in the successful establishment of learner support groups. These could include such considerations as:

- **their experience of consciously using interpersonal skills**

- **their stage of development in being autonomous and independent learners**

- **their individual learning style**

- **their motivation for, and commitment to, learning**

- **their experience of working in small groups**

- **their experience of peer support**

- **their level of confidence**

- **if you are using IT as a means of communication, their experience of this.**

You could address some of the above issues by identifying your own expectations in advance. Going back to the defined aims and purpose of the student support group will help you with this.

What do you see as the role of students in your learning context? Two examples are given.
Role
Sharing in learning
Receiving knowledge

Some of the roles you have identified will be more relevant to students' roles within the context of the whole tutor group and some will be more relevant within the context of student support groups. You may find it helpful to negotiate students' roles with the students themselves, within a framework which you plan in advance. This will give them the opportunity of identifying their needs and expectations and you the opportunity of negotiating how those needs could be met within the constraints and opportunities available.

SUMMARY

This chapter has covered the following areas:

- *The broad aims and purpose of student support groups*

- *Relevance to the unit, course or programme*

- *The role of the tutor*

- *The role of the student.*

Before moving to the next chapter, you might find it helpful to consider the above areas in relation to the student support group within your own teaching and learning context.

2
ADVANCE PLANNING - SETTING UP

2.1 How will the student support groups be structured?
2.2 What will the student support groups be doing?
2.3 What structured support materials could be useful?
2.4 What could you do at the first session?
2.5 Summary

Once you have decided on the purpose of using student support groups, the next step is to consider the practicalities of setting them up. The more planning you can do in advance, the more effective the process will be.

This chapter will consider the following questions:

- **How will the student support groups be structured?**

- **What will the student support groups be doing?**

- **What structured support materials could be useful?**

- **What could you do at the first session?**

2.1 HOW WILL THE STUDENT SUPPORT GROUPS BE STRUCTURED?

2.1.1 Number in a group

Generally four or five is a good number of people to work together. Evidence suggests that three and six may be less productive and more difficult for the students to co-ordinate. If attendance is likely to be variable, however, larger numbers could be better. The same would be true if students were working at a distance, through computer conferencing for example.

You may not feel that the term 'Student Support Group' is appropriate to your group of learners. The term you choose will depend on the aims that you have identified. Other possible names are listed on page 2.

2.1.2 Forming the support groups

• You can decide randomly (place in the room) or more selectively (alphabetically), or use a mixture of both methods. It is worth considering whether you want to identify criteria, for example, encouraging mixed groups in terms of gender, subject, experience, age or common interest groups, such as mature students. Experience suggests that smaller tutor groups consisting of twelve or less students will be more reluctant to split into support groups. In this instance, it may be preferable to randomly select the group, particularly if a few of the students are already known to each other.

• Students can decide on their own criteria for support group membership, for example, according to interest, age, gender, background and geographical location. Icebreakers and initial activities are needed to provide a framework for students to do this. They can decide on group membership based on these criteria. You have an important role here. Some ideas are provided below and in 2.4 (p31)

Place

Using the two maps below, students work in groups drawing lines indicating where they have travelled in their lives through moving house and holidays. It is useful for each group to have different coloured pens. This is a really good way of getting people to share information about themselves in a short period of time.

Human Bingo

Each and every box must be signed by the given number of people you are asked to find

Find someone who has a cat	Find someone you can swap an item of clothing with	Find someone who is taller than you are
Find someone who likes taking risks	Find someone who lives close to you	Find someone who knows about a subject that you'd like to know more about
Find someone who has a similar taste in music	Find someone who has been to the same or a similar place on holiday	Find someone wearing an earring
Find two people around the same age as you	Find someone who's done something adventurous/exciting in the last year	Find someone who likes the same colour
Find two people who watch the same soaps on TV	Find someone who enjoys the same or a similar subject to you	Find someone who has a teddy bear
Find someone who is looking forward to the course		

Human Bingo

Using the 'bingo' sheet on the previous page, learners move around the room and find someone who fulfils one of the requirements in one of the boxes. For example, 'has a cat'. This is signed by the person who has a cat. The students move on until all the boxes are signed, and they therefore have a 'full house'. Alternatively, see how it goes and start with a line. It is important to adapt the topics in the boxes to suit your own group. Learners need encouragement to try to talk to as many people as possible.

Simple Group Tasks

These can be used to encourage co-operation and sharing and can be tailor-made to a particular course subject or unit. Examples might include:

• **a small group agreement on an ideal menu**

• **a small group presentation on how to tackle a project or assignment**

• **a small group response to a homework question.**

The important thing is that the activity caters for notions of consensus and compromise as well as introducing simple issues relevant to the course of study.

2.1.3 Duration of the student support groups

Consider when you will expect the student support groups to form:

• **from the first week onwards?**

• **from the third or fourth week?**

• **during a unit?**

and how long you will expect them to continue:

• **over 3 – 4 units?**

• **over a whole programme?**

• **during a term/semester**

Even if you plan on the student support groups working only for the duration of a unit, you might find that if it works effectively, it may well continue informally throughout the programme.

2.1.4 Changes in group membership

You might decide that changes in group membership will not be considered during the unit or semester. Another option is to build into your planning a change in the second semester or following each unit. This links in with the selection of student support group members. Examples of practice include:

- **random selection in the first term/semester; student choice of support group members in the second term/semester**

- **student and/or tutor decision on criteria for selection at the beginning of each unit, and membership decided on that basis**

- **changing support group membership at the beginning of each year**

- **changes made in support group membership on the basis of review.**

It is worth incorporating interim reviews within the structure whether or not you choose to provide an opportunity for support group membership to change. Chapter 3 on *Monitoring, Support and Review* may give you some ideas.

2.1.5 Tutor-led sessions

It is worth considering whether or not students will need to work, or at least be in contact, outside of the session time. Session time can mean any tutor contact time, including class time, computer or telephone conferencing, or the tutor meeting with students outside of the institution. When and how often will you want the students to meet in support groups outside of session time? Will this be a requirement of the course/programme? Even if support groups meet and work only outside session time, without the input of the tutor, in order for support groups to work successfully, it is useful to spend some time with the whole tutor group on:

- **aims and purpose of the student support group**

- **expectations – this might include discussion on hopes and fears**

- **sharing experiences of working in student support groups**

- **group work skills and issues, team building and problem-solving, for example**

- **ground rules – this might include attendance, timing, confidentiality and communication.**

See below for an example of an agreement made between tutor and students.

Ground Rules

We are working towards an open and inclusive learning environment, based on mutual respect and equal worth

in which:-

only one person speaks at once

we value listening

a fair share of time is given to all

there is equality of opportunity

there is freedom to 'be yourself'

there is security and support

there is honesty

there is the scope to challenge or confront

there is the opportunity for each person to say what they want,
think and feel

there is humour
and
we all enjoy ourselves

we also intend to start and finish on time – and have the coffee breaks

All of this can be implemented in more flexible teaching/learning contexts through other means of communication using, for example, IT and Open Learning resources. Spending session time on support group work doesn't mean that you will have less time to spend on teaching the subject; the student support groups could spend some of their time working through the subject, both within and outside session time.

2.1.6 Administrative arrangements

If students are working without you, whether or not during session time, you need to consider administrative arrangements. For example:

- **Do you have enough administrative support, as this approach can lead you to require more materials and more effective methods of communication?**
- **What communication system will be used between students and between you and the students? E-mail, computer conferencing, noticeboard, pigeonholes, letters, telephone, fax?**
- **Do students have access to e-mail, computer conferencing or fax facilities?**
- **When will you be available for students and administrative staff to contact?**
- **Are you able to provide a space/room for student support groups to meet outside of the session time, if required?**

These are a list of questions you might ask students to help you organise administrative arrangements. Tick those relevant to you and add others below.	
How will you contact each other?	☐
What is the best way for you to contact the tutor?	☐
Will you need a room to meet in?	☐
When will you need a room?	☐
What facilities will you need?	☐
What written information or resource materials will you need to help you?	☐
Are you registered for e mail and/or computer conferencing?	☐

2.2 WHAT WILL THE STUDENT SUPPORT GROUPS BE DOING?

It is worth defining from the outset the activities you would like the student support groups to undertake. You might then ask them to identify, in their support groups, other activities related to their own group and individual needs. This can form the basis of a group contract. Some activities might include:

- **sharing library books, articles, contacts and other resources**

- **reading each other's drafts of assignments and giving feedback**

- **practising/rehearsing a presentation/interview in a supportive environment**

- **allocating specific tasks related to a coursework activity and meeting to share results**

- **supporting each other; e.g. maintain contact, collect handouts etc.**

- **clarifying issues relating to the course and/or work/placement role**

- **reviewing learning and progress.**

Whatever activities you identify, whether they are planned, student-negotiated and/or spontaneous, they need to be seen to be valued. How could you demonstrate that these are valued?

Some ideas are included below:

- **ensuring that issues relating to support group work are discussed in sessions**

- **providing an opportunity for students to give feedback on how the support groups have worked**

- **providing an opportunity for individuals to share their experiences in mixed groups**

- **incorporating course work within support group activities**

- **having support group tutorials, either face to face or through telephone or computer conferencing**

- **providing constructive and positive feedback to support groups**

- **incorporating some of the work completed in support groups within the assessment of the unit**

- **informally asking individuals how the support group is going**

- **incorporating feedback on support groups within the evaluation of the unit/programme.**

Incorporating some of the work completed in support groups within the sessions is only one way to demonstrate that you value the activities/work of the student support groups. You might, for example, consider how the activities relate to the learning outcomes of the programme or unit.

Please list the tasks or activities you want your learners to undertake and indicate which of these you think are linked to the learning outcomes of the course/programme.	
Tasks/Activities	**Links?**

2.2.1 Group contract

You might want to encourage each student support group to create a group contract, in which members agree on how they will operate as a group. This can help students identify their own roles and responsibilities, and may avoid future difficulties.

It is worth providing a framework for learners to negotiate their own contract. (See over for examples). You could give them some ground rules and encourage the students to negotiate and add others. You might consider providing a problem-solving exercise which includes case studies of possible difficulties they may come up against, such as what if one person doesn't 'pull their weight'.

Support Group – Learning Contract

This contract agrees the contribution of each group member to completing the assignment/task. Please identify which sub-tasks each group member will complete, and by when.

Assignment title

Name	Sub-task	Date for completion

signed

date   tutor

Support Group – Initial Learning Contract

As a group, complete the following. Make sure that everyone has their own copy and review/amend as appropriate through the year.

1.   What are your current aims? (i.e. how do you see your role as a group?)

_____

_____

_____

2.   What do you want to achieve and by when?

_____

_____

_____

3.   What will you use to help you? (e.g. people, resources).

_____

_____

_____

4.   How often do you intend to meet?

_____

_____

_____

5.   Discuss and list the ground rules for the group.

_____

_____

_____

6.   How will you monitor and review the group's progress?

_____

_____

_____

2.3 WHAT STRUCTURED SUPPORT MATERIALS COULD BE USEFUL?

Students usually need a structured framework to help them get started in working more independently, whatever the identified purpose of the student support group. Support materials, such as information sheets and booklets, providing clear information can play a key role here. They can also help to save you time dealing with minor queries.

2.3.1 Information sheets

Information sheets will include information the students may need, preferably supported verbally. Some examples of information which students find helpful in written form are listed below.

Please tick those which you consider relevant to your own teaching/learning situation. Add any others you consider important.	
Course title, syllabus description, aims and learning outcomes	☐
Tutors' names, numbers and availability	☐
Broad aims and suggested activities of the support group	☐
Role of the tutor during the course and in relation to the support group	☐
Overall work requirements and assessment requirements (as appropriate)	☐
Attendance requirements for the course and for the support groups	☐
Duration – how long the students are expected to be in the support groups	☐
Basic information on communication and learning through IT (see References)	☐
Reading list	☐
List of students' names. During the icebreaking sessions, students can make notes against each name if they wish, noting common interests, for example.	☐

Examples of guidelines and structured handouts are provided below.

Support Group

Guidelines

At each meeting you need to decide:

- **the full amount of time available**

- **the amount of time each individual will have**

- **the amount of group time you will allocate**

- **the group agenda**

- **who will keep an eye on the time. This may rotate during the meeting.**

It is useful to decide on a contract or ground rules for the group. These will be particular to your group but may include issues around:

- **confidentiality**

- **punctuality**

- **communication – in meetings and between meetings**

- **the role of the group**

- **commitment**

- **monitoring and review: How and when you will review the group process. For example, you might decide to briefly review the previous meeting at the beginning of the following meeting. Your contract will therefore continually evolve and develop.**

Use the initial learning contract sheet as a starting point.

Individually write your own review of your learning and development within the group. This can form part of your portfolio.

If you have any questions or issues that you cannot resolve as a group, nominate someone to contact your group tutor or arrange a support group tutorial.

Support Group

Starting Up

Name and Contact Numbers:

Aims/area/issues common to all members:

Time and place of first meeting:

Individual aims/agenda for first meeting:

Resources/action needed for first meeting:

2.3.2 Skill development materials

Gower has published "The Student Skills Guide" (Drew and Bingham, 1997), designed to support students in their academic, personal and professional development. The chapters are designed as student-centred interactive materials, offering information and suggestions, and using a similar approach to that demonstrated in this book. They aim to raise student self-awareness of particular skills, encouraging them to reflect on strengths and weaknesses in order to further develop in that skill area.

Student support groups could effectively work through some of these areas with tutor support. They are best used in relation to a specific task or assignment, at a time when they are most relevant. *Group work* and *Negotiating and assertiveness* are particularly useful for students to work through in support groups.

Skill areas which are directly relevant to course activities/assignments	Skill areas which are directly underpinning skills
Essay writing	Identifying strengths, improving skills
Group work	Coping with pressure
Gathering and using information	Managing yourself and your time
Report writing	Negotiating and assertiveness
Revision and examination techniques	Reflection
Oral presentation	Critical analysis

2.4 WHAT COULD YOU DO AT THE FIRST SESSION?

This is an opportunity to set the scene and ensure that learners have a clear idea of the purpose of student support groups and what is expected of them.

2.4.1 Group development

Tuckman and Jenson (1977) suggested that all groups go through four main stages in their development – the stages of *forming, storming, norming and performing*. All the stages are relevant regardless of whether the group is led by the tutor or whether it is peer-led, as in a student support group. You may consider discussing these stages with the students. This information could provide a framework for a review where the students can work out at what stage they feel they are, in the group with you and in their support groups.

2.4.2 The forming stage – Group introductions and formation

A group of people meeting for the first time is more like a collection of highly stressed individuals with their own personal fears, expectations, shyness and feelings of disorientation than a group. These are the characteristics of the forming stage. At the first meeting, therefore, a group is unlikely to be able to take in complex information or carry out demanding tasks. They will be dependent on you as their tutor, to reassure, organise and explain.

The following activities can be useful to help students relax, promote communication and channel the potential hostility which stress and anxiety can create. They can provide an opportunity for students to feel more comfortable with each other and help them form and/or work in support groups.

In planning initial activities, including icebreakers, it is worth thinking about whether you will participate or not. You may choose to join in or remain on the sidelines as an observer. Instructions need to be clear and students need to be encouraged to express the level of self disclosure and participation they feel comfortable with. The issue of confidentiality is crucial and needs to be addressed from the outset.

Introductions

Students introduce themselves to each other either in pairs or threes. Before completing this exercise and going back to the larger or whole group, they need to agree on what information they are prepared to share. In the larger or whole group, rather than each individual introducing him/herself, each student introduces the person he/she has been sharing with to the group.

Four Corners

This is an effective exercise to do with large groups and can be used specifically to help enable students form support groups. Learners are asked to go to a corner of the room according to an identified theme and/or interest which you call out. They spend 3–4 minutes telling each other their names before the next interest is identified. It is useful to provide themes which will help groupings within the class identify each other. Geographical location, for example, may be one of the criteria you or learners will want to choose to help decide on support group formation. This should be done quite quickly. If you get an enthusiastic response, it is worth asking the learners for ideas. The following are examples.

Favourite drink – tea, coffee, juice, alcohol
Birthdays – January–March, April–June, July–September, October–December
Residence – Sheffield, South Yorkshire apart from Sheffield, Derbyshire, Nottinghamshire
Favourite holiday – sea, mountains, country, town
Hobbies – arts, crafts, sports, other

Groupings

A similar exercise to Four Corners can be done with people raising their hands, using any criteria from who's got a cat, to who lives in Sheffield.

Hopes and Fears

In small groups, students list their hopes and fears. Some of these, if agreed, can be shared in the larger group. This is a good way of encouraging co-operation in a new group, giving students an unpressurised chance to express how they feel, and it provides you with some valuable information.

Human Bingo

See Section 2.1.2 (p19)

Feelings

This is a useful exercise to help express and allay fears and anxieties present at the beginning of a course of study. Ask learners to individually complete the handout below, writing down one feeling in each of the four sections of the box, for example, 'I feel nervous', 'I feel anxious'. When this has been completed, ask each person to circle the feeling in the box that stands out most for them. Then, in twos or threes, encourage them to share their feelings, the reasons behind them and any ideas they have on what would help allay their anxieties. Encourage them to share their ideas in the larger group.

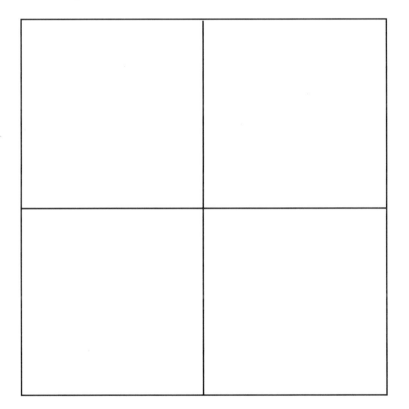

At the *forming* stage, the learners are concerned about what is expected of them, what is going to happen, whether they will be accepted and whether their needs will be met. You can alleviate their concerns by defining and structuring procedures and by identifying the norms of the group. One way this can be done is by giving your learners a handout which explains the aims and suggested activities of a student support group. It is useful to go through this with them to check understanding, and, as appropriate, to negotiate further aims and/or activities. You may want to provide information on your role as a tutor, the support you will provide to the groups both within and outside session time. Your initial information sheets (Section 2.3.1) will be very useful at this stage.

2.4.3 The storming stage

At the storming stage, learners can more directly express concern about leadership, membership and authority. Individuals may attempt to dominate discussion, to ridicule others and they may even divide into camps. Attacking the tutor, for example, through having a common cause e.g. dissatisfaction with the course, can give the group its first sense of common identity. There might equally be attacks on the course content or methods. This is a normal phase in group development.

Learners may be involved in:

- **A swing towards independence or a return to a more passive role, resisting taking responsibility for their own learning.**
- **Disagreements and conflicts. Support group members may attack the perceived leader. Relationships, however, are often established through a cycle of becoming friendly, establishing independence through disagreement and conflict and then giving a commitment to the relationship.**

2.4.4 The norming stage

At the *norming* stage the group members, having found their 'position' in the group, may look for ways of coming together and looking for a common identity. Some of the feeling of belonging comes from the experience of working through the conflicts of the previous stage. Thus each member may feel s/he has a role in the group and appreciate the role that others play. This may form a large part in the 'claim' for membership in the group. At this stage, however, any individual disagreement or challenge to group decisions may be interpreted as a sign of 'rocking the boat', and, as a result, the group may close ranks to maintain its new-found identity.

At this stage, the group members are more likely to want to know how others think and feel about things, are more likely to ask for feedback, as well as to listen to the feedback received. This is a time when students are taking responsibility for the goals, procedures and for other members. You may feel that the support groups are more easily managed and take this as an appropriate time to re-negotiate their main priorities and time management.

2.4.5 The performing stage

At the *performing* stage, the group is at its most productive, being more aware of its power and potential. As well as the 'group feeling' of the previous stage, individuals are now seen again as individuals and accepted as such. Thus, differences of opinion and challenges to decisions on how the group operates are not seen as 'rocking the boat' but are listened to and valued as a way of improving the effectiveness of the group. This trust allows individuals to take risks. It enables them, for example, by trying out new behaviours and talking about the relationships in the group/support group, to build confidence in themselves and in the possibilities of team work.

At this stage, the group collaborates effectively and can deal with conflicts in constructive ways. Your role becomes that of consultant or resource.

SUMMARY

This chapter has covered the following areas :

- *Number in student support groups*

- *Duration of the student support groups*

- *Administrative arrangements*

- *Structured support materials*

- *Ice breakers/initial activities*

- *Support group contract*

- *First session*

- *Support group activities*

- *Group development.*

Before moving to the next chapter, you might find it useful to check that you have made the relevant decisions in relation to setting up your support groups.

3
ADVANCE PLANNING - MONITORING, SUPPORT AND REVIEW

3.1 Why do you want to monitor and support student support groups?
3.2 How will you organise the monitoring and support process?
3.3 What will you monitor and review?
3.4 What methods will you use to review?
3.5 Summary

Your role does not end with setting up the student support groups, but continues and develops into monitoring and supporting the progress of the groups.

This chapter will consider the following questions:

- **Why do you want to monitor and support student support groups?**

- **How will you organise the monitoring and support process?**

- **What will you monitor and review?**

- **What methods will you use to review?**

3.1 WHY DO YOU WANT TO MONITOR AND SUPPORT THE STUDENT SUPPORT GROUPS?

Please tick the reasons that you consider important and add any additional reasons below.	
To provide opportunities for students to tell you about successes	☐
To provide an opportunity for students to air their views both as individuals and group members	☐
To check that students are supporting each other effectively	☐
To provide opportunities for students to tell you about any difficulties	☐
To gain feedback on your role, checking that you are providing what they need	☐
To check that students are meeting the attendance requirement	☐
To check that students understand the aims and activities	☐
To check that there are sufficient and appropriate resources e.g. computers	☐
To ascertain the needs and support of this particular group of students, (which may be different from those of the previous year)	☐
To check that the communication system is adequate for students' needs	☐
To check that the groups are achieving the intended learning outcomes	☐
To check that all students are participating	☐

Having identified your reasons, you might ask the students what they consider important to focus on and add their ideas to your list. You might ask them to consider these on a systematic basis. This will also enable them to monitor their own progress and identify their successes. It may also result in additional aims and/or activities being identified.

An example of a structure for the first meeting and following the first meeting is given below.

First Meeting - Support Group

You have 1 hour to work in your support groups. Here is a suggested structure detailing how you could use that time effectively. Please nominate a timekeeper, ensure everyone has an equal turn, and nominate someone to report back. You do not need to hand this in.

1. Progress on the group task - to produce a report.

What issues have been raised?

What needs to be done next? Who will do what? What, if any, support is needed?

group member	task	support needed

2. Progress on individual assignments

What issues have been raised?

What does each person have to do next? What support is needed?

name	task	support

3. Progress on learning record/self-evaluation

What does each group member need to do next? What support is needed?

group member	task	support needed

4. Please list any specific questions for the tutor

5. Does the group need tutorial time?　　　　　　**Yes/No**

If yes, what would you like to cover?

6. Do any individuals need tutorial time?　　　　　**Yes/No**

If yes, what would you like to cover?

Support Group –
Individual Review following first meeting

After the first meeting, use this pro-forma to help you consider your own ideas on the support group. Decide what you will share at your next support group meeting.

Name:

Your original aim/s for the first meeting:

Was this achieved? YES/NO

What particular aspects of the meeting helped/supported you?

What aspect/s of the meeting would you like to change?

Are there any parts of the contract/ground rules you would like to develop/add to?
If so, what?

What do you hope to get out of the next meeting?

What support or questions do you need to be answered by your tutor?

3.2 HOW WILL YOU ORGANISE THE MONITORING AND SUPPORT PROCESS?

Monitoring is a continuous process. It is worth organising this process in advance, ensuring the use of simple and effective mechanisms related to the nature of your group of students. Some support groups have found it useful to keep their own minutes which can be shared with anyone who is absent from a meeting and used as a starting point for the following meeting. In particular, it is important to decide what form of recording and communication you will use to monitor, support, provide feedback and to help you produce an action plan.

Please tick the examples that you consider relevant. You may have others you can add.	
Attendance records	☐
Tutorial records (individual/support group)	☐
Action plans	☐
Review sheets (individual/support group) (see below for examples)	☐
Individual learning records	☐
Individual/support group diary	☐
A course/unit noticeboard	☐
E-mail	☐
A postal system	☐
Telephone	☐
Individual tutorial	☐
Support group tutorial	☐
Learning contract (individual/support group)	☐
Computer conferencing	☐
Video conferencing	☐

Some examples of review sheets are given below:

Support Group

Individual Review

After your group has made the presentation, complete this individual review sheet to help you focus on how you are functioning in the group to complete a task, and to focus on what developments you have made with your presentation skills.

Your behaviour

Score yourself using the following scale, where 1 is 'very helpful' and 4 is 'very unhelpful'. **Try to be honest with yourself.**

	1	2	3	4	
Listening to others, asking for clarification					Interrupting, putting others down
Expressing relevant views positively					Being negative, disruptive, being irrelevant
Contributing equally					Keeping quiet/dominating
Asking what others think about your contributions					Unconcerned about others views
Pulling your weight, doing an equal part of the work					Letting others do the work, not turning up
Meeting deadlines					Missing deadlines

(Adapted from Drew/Bingham (1997) 'Student Skills Guide')

Is there anything else you think you should note about your behaviour?

What aspects of your behaviour can you work on during the next meeting/task to improve your group working skills?

Support Group Work

What has helped you work more as a team?

Tick those you have done and those you would like to do	Have done	Would like
get to know each other	☐	☐
do something social together	☐	☐
carry out a task together	☐	☐
disclose personal information about yourself	☐	☐
express feelings about being in the group	☐	☐
identify your individual skills which may be useful to the group	☐	☐
identify your strengths and potential weaknesses as a group	☐	☐
identify your individual preferences about how you like to work with others	☐	☐
do something creative together such as build or draw something	☐	☐
play a game or have fun together	☐	☐

Other ideas:

	Have done	Would like
_____	☐	☐
_____	☐	☐
_____	☐	☐
_____	☐	☐
_____	☐	☐
_____	☐	☐
_____	☐	☐
_____	☐	☐

Support Group Work

What has hindered you from working more as a team?

Tick those that you feel have happened and discuss as a group

don't join in ☐

allow an individual to dominate ☐

prevented from joining in ☐

avoid any expression of feelings ☐

refuse to set yourselves any task or goal ☐

don't find out about each other ☐

don't disclose anything about yourself ☐

criticise without being constructive ☐

don't listen to each other ☐

show no interest ☐

Others: _____

_____

_____

_____

_____

_____

_____

_____

3.2.1 Tutorial activity

There are two different models of tutorial support that can be used as part of the monitoring process.

• **individual tutorial - this may not be an option with large numbers**

• **support group tutorial.**

Both of these could be conducted through e-mail and computer/video conferencing.

With both models, it is worth considering who will decide on the agenda for the tutorial. Time is used effectively when this can be planned in advance, by both students and tutors. You can provide a pro-forma relating to progress, including the criteria for monitoring. This can be completed by students, both as a support group and individually, prior to the tutorial. It is helpful to provide a space on the pro-forma for students to outline issues they want to discuss with you, before you meet. This can be a useful exercise, providing a focus for both the support group and the individual to review their progress. The photocopied completed pro-forma can form part of your recording system for monitoring progress and act as a contract between you and the student/s. Examples are given below.

Group Tutorial

1. Names: Students   Tutor

                                                      Date

2. Issues to be raised/discussed:

3. Action to be taken:

name	action and by when	signed
Tutor		
Students		

Individual Tutorial

1. Name: Student   Tutor

2. Issues to be raised/discussed:

3. Action to be taken:

Tutor		by when?
Student		

Signed: tutor   student   date:

Another issue for tutorials is when and how often to have them and whether to make them compulsory. If voluntary, it is often the case that those who need most support will not attend. It is therefore worthwhile building tutorials into the planned programme. Both you and the group/individual can then negotiate an action plan to be reviewed at a given date. If a common theme or difficulty emerges in tutorials, you might decide to deal with it in a group session.

The time set aside for tutorials is not wasted and can be effectively structured to incorporate a variety of activities. It can be used by students to plan for their tutorial, have the tutorial and complete a specific given activity to be reviewed at the following group session. This structured approach could be used, particularly at the initial stages, to enhance the value of tutorial time and to further support group activity.

3.3 WHAT WILL YOU MONITOR AND REVIEW?

Whatever the aims of the student support group and whether or not the process involves assessment, the progress and process of support group work, however informal, should be included within the evaluation of the programme or unit. This not only values its contribution, but may provide you with further insights as to how the support group work fits into the programme and how it could be developed further.

The processes of monitoring and review form the basis of any evaluation programme. It is helpful to distinguish between the two:

- *Monitoring* is about checking progress. It is the process of gathering information on a *continuing* basis over a period of time. This is difficult to do in retrospect.

- *Review* is about taking stock. This involves a *periodic* assessment of progress and achievement. Interim reviews inform the final review or evaluation of the unit.

What aspects of the following do you need to monitor on a continuous basis (checking progress)? Which do you need to review (i.e. taking stock)?		
Focus	Monitor	Review
Are the aims being achieved?		
Are the learning outcomes being met?		
What unanticipated learning is taking place?		
What learning has taken place?		
Are individuals progressing/having difficulties?		
Is the role of the support group changing?		
Does my role need to change? If so, how?		
Are group members supporting each other? If so, how?		
In what ways are support group members not supporting each other?		
What activities are the support group members involved in?		

On-going monitoring and interim review can give you the flexibility to make changes as the need arises and enable you to respond to developments. You may find it useful to build in time for a specific interim review as well as a final review of the unit or programme. It is helpful to give students the opportunity to give feedback both as support group members and as individuals. When you are monitoring and supporting students and reviewing the unit/programme, what will you be looking at in particular? To some extent this will be determined by the aims you identified when setting up the student support groups initially.

3.4 WHAT METHODS WILL YOU USE TO REVIEW?

Time for review needs to be set aside on a systematic yet manageable basis. There are many ways to organise reviews. The purpose of review is to reflect on what has happened, clarify the present situation and identify what might happen next.

Any of the following suggestions could be used to help you review the support group work process. These can also be used as part of your monitoring process. The choice will be dependent upon your aims, your relationship with your students and their level of confidence with you and with each other.

- **The Good, the Bad and the Funny**

Summary: Play in a round or circle. Each member of the group describes something good, something bad and something funny.

Use: Could be used alone or as a starting point for reviewing activity/discussion, i.e. after everyone has had a turn, you should have a good idea of things the group need to discuss.

Variations: Different headings could be used, e.g. the hard, the easy, the interesting etc.

- **Unfinished Sentences**

Summary: Each member of the group completes an unfinished sentence relating to the focus of the review. It is probably best to bring in a rule that no one can repeat other people's endings.

Uses: A good starting point for discussion.

Preparation: Prepare a list of unfinished sentences.

Variations: After each round someone else introduces the new sentence beginning. This can be done using flipchart paper where the heading is the beginning of a sentence and group members complete them below using pen or post-its. Examples of some unfinished sentences include:
Something I'll remember about my support group is ...
One thing I didn't like about this activity was ...
If someone told me they were thinking of joining the group ...
The most important thing I've learned so far is ...

Sentence completion and statements can be written on different coloured cards. These are collected in and redistributed so that other group members can then read them. This ensures that individual contributions remain anonymous. Similar activities can be used at the beginning of a programme, perhaps recording participants' hopes, fears and expectations. These can be collated and recorded and used at later stages to remind learners of their starting points and the progress made.

- **Drawings/Posters**

Summary: Individuals produce drawings representing how they feel about the unit/support group, how they see themselves in the unit/support group, how it is affecting or has affected them. In small groups, each person briefly describes and interprets their picture.

Use: Drawing can often bring out issues for the individual (s)he may not have realised. The exercise is about ideas, not standards of artistry, and it is important to point this out, particularly for those who feel less confident about their artistic skills. You will need to listen to the group discussion while students are working to reinforce this point as necessary.

Variations: The drawings could make a 'graffiti' wall. One or two words could be provided for each drawing and used to initiate discussion. Groups could also produce a joint drawing/poster. Again, it is important that this is discussed.

- **Post-its**

Summary: Individuals write down on separate post-its positive and negative aspects of the work in support groups. They put these on the wall.

Variations: Group members can categorise them on the wall in order to highlight the issues raised.

- **Questionnaires**

Summary: Questionnaires relating to the support group work can be completed by each member of the group (see below for an example).It is worth noting that universities use a lot of questionnaires and students may not be responsive. A short, well-focused questionnaire works best. Small, mixed groups then get together to discuss their responses and issues raised. Key issues agreed by each support group can then be aired by a representative.

Uses: Provides both an individual and support group review.

Variation: This can be done in turn, based on the issue. For example, if the first group raised the issue of the environment, other groups would be asked for their contribution related to this (if any). The tutor writes down the issues raised to provide a focus.

Support Group Review

What did you feel were the advantages of being in a support group?

What were the disadvantages?

If you encountered any problems as a group, what were they and how did you overcome them?

What was good about the support group?

How could tutor support be improved?

On the whole, do you think that being in a support group has been useful? YES/NO
If yes, why?

If no, why not?

Would you work in a support group again?

Review Meetings

Review meetings can play a key part in managing the inclusion of all of those who may have a direct interest in an area of development. They may involve groups of staff, staff and students, or students. People who have been involved in the process of identifying any necessary next steps will be more likely to have a commitment to carrying these out. Representatives can be invited from tutor groups and /or support groups.

Advantages:

- **existing meetings, or directed time, can be set aside for a process of review so that other time is not intruded upon**

- **issues are openly shared and discussed and participants are able to be active in the process of establishing conclusions**

- **a lot of ground can be covered quickly enabling more in depth study to focus on issues identified as requiring this**

- **the process of clarifying issues and ideas can be satisfying and give everyone the sense of moving forward**

- **if problems are revealed and shared there is the possibility of shared commitment to take appropriate action**

- **it is possible to establish some picture of what a whole staff and student group is feeling about development in a short period of time**

- **there is opportunity for definitions and conclusions to be fully discussed**

- **it provides an opportunity to value students' opinions and to share progress on student support.**

Disadvantages:

- **difficulties in relationships may make some people unwilling to be open about their ideas or opinions**

- **individuals may dominate a group discussion and push it in certain directions**

- **only the perceptions of the moment can be captured and other outside events may affect the mood of the meeting in a way that influences the outcome. Timing is therefore important and the event needs to be carefully structured and managed.**

SUMMARY

This chapter has covered the following:

- *Reasons for monitoring student support groups*

- *Organising the monitoring of the support process*

- *Tutorial activity*

- *Focus of monitoring and review*

- *Methods of reviewing*

Before moving on to the next chapter, you might like to complete the following summary grid in relation to your own teaching/learning situation and your work with support groups.		
Support Groups	**What?**	**How?**
Monitoring and Support		
Review and Evaluation		

4
ADVANCE PLANNING - ASSESSMENT

4.1 Will you use assessment with support groups?
4.2 What will you assess?
4.3 Who will assess?
4.4 How will marks be allocated?
4.5 What evidence can be provided?
4.6 Summary

It is worth considering whether the work undertaken in student support groups can be counted as part of the assessment of the programme. As with all aspects of developing student support groups, assessment needs advance planning.

This chapter will consider the following questions:

- **Will you use assessment with support groups?**

- **What will you assess?**

- **Who will assess?**

- **How will you allocate marks?**

- **What evidence can be provided?**

4.1 WILL YOU USE ASSESSMENT WITH SUPPORT GROUPS?

You may choose to use support groups as a mechanism solely for peer support, and so not involve assessment. Assessment driven group work may affect the supportive nature of the support group work. It is worth prioritising your aims to help you decide on the appropriateness and nature of assessment. With more emphasis placed on assessment, the peer support may be devalued and/or undermined.

Some involvement in assessment, however, can give the work of a support group more value and can act as an incentive for students. It is worth thinking about the relationship between the work students do in support groups and assessment. Assessment can influence how students operate in groups and can affect the learning process itself. Many students regard group-assessed work with suspicion, feeling that they are working towards individual awards, with classification/marks determined by individual effort. They may view the assessment of group projects with suspicion, believing that it might involve factors beyond their immediate control. (Drew and Parsons, 1995).

4.2 WHAT WILL YOU ASSESS?

Your purpose for setting up groups will determine what you assess. If learning about teamwork is an aim, then students will need to record and monitor the group process. If developing skills is an aim, then students need to monitor their own personal skills.

Are you going to assess...	
Academic understanding and knowledge, however achieved, whether individually with support or as a group?	☐
The presentation of that learning, either oral or written?	☐
The way each group functions - the group process?	☐
The skills each individual student has acquired through the group work process?	☐

Whatever and however you choose to assess, students need to be given clear, written information about the assessment process, the criteria by which they will be judged and a breakdown of how the marks will be allocated. It may be helpful to discuss the assessment rationale and process with the students.

4.3 WHO WILL ASSESS?

4.3.1 Peer-assessment

Students need to be introduced to peer-assessment gradually, to gain confidence and experience. They need to develop a sophisticated approach e.g. does the extrovert really contribute the most, or the quiet member the least? You could use a secret ballot. This could help overcome some of the difficulties.

Benefits	*Difficulties*
• **encourages students to reflect and analyse**	• **students manipulating the system to give each other high marks**
• **encourages students to learn from each other**	• **students allocating the marks equally, so as to be 'fair'**
• **gives students experience of giving and receiving feedback**	• **students not feeling comfortable with criticising others**
• **it could reduce the tutor's marking load - but it may not**	• **students feeling that it is the tutor's responsibility and what s/he is paid for**
	• **marks may be influenced by gender, age, disability or racial bias**

You could use peer-assessment:

- **as a proportion of all the marks e.g. for assessment of the group process**

- **for the purpose of giving and receiving feedback and gaining experience rather than as an assessment method for awarding marks e.g. to comment on each other's work, and allow re-drafting before it is handed in for assessment.**

An example is given below:

Group Work
Peer-Assessment Sheet

....has contributed to the group in the following ways.

Signed..   Date.........................

Tutor's name..

Ratings:
4 = a major strength
3 = a strength
2 = usually adequate
1 = a priority for development

✓

	rating			
The group member's contribution to the group was to ...	1	2	3	4
be a leader in meetings				
complete tasks on time				
do his/her share of the work				
communicate effectively				
provide ideas				
participate and contribute				
support and encourage others				
express his/her feelings openly and appropriately				
constructively criticise				
be flexible and adaptable				
be confident				
enjoy it				

Feedback can help students develop and learn, either as a group or individually. Students will need clear guidelines on how to give and receive feedback. As part of their personal and professional development, they need the opportunity to practise giving feedback before using peer assessment as a method.

Written and verbal feedback according to Boud (1988) should be :

* **realistic**   * **direct**

* **specific**   * **positive**

* **sensitive to the goals of the person**   * **non-comparative**

* **timely**   * **unaffected by your feelings**

* **non-judgmental**

4.3.2 Self-assessment

Self-assessment is not the same as self-marking (Boud,1995). Students need the opportunity to practise the skill before using marks to count towards their accreditation.

Benefits

* **encourages students to develop their reflective skills – raises self-awareness.**

* **encourages students to be more self critical and able to evaluate themselves and their performance.**

Difficulties

* **students may need training in how to self-assess (clear criteria and guidance will help). This suggests heavy initial tutor input.**

* **some students may lack confidence in their own judgements. Again, race, age, disability or gender may be influential.**

* **how do tutors ensure accuracy? Can self-assessment be measured?**

You could use self-assessment:

* **as one aspect of the whole assessment, e.g. as part of an individual student's evaluation of the whole project**

* **in a portfolio of skill development, to aid skill development**

* **as a basis for discussion e.g. the student could self-assess and the group peer-assess. The two are then compared, but not marked.**

* **students could be given the marking criteria for a report and mark themselves, then compare it with the tutor assessment.**

An example is given below:

Group Work
Self-Assessment Sheet

Name.. ... ...   Date.......................

Tutor's name......................................

Ratings:
4 = a major strength   2 = usually adequate
3 = a strength   1 = a priority for development

✔

My contribution to the group was to ...	rating			
	1	2	3	4
be a leader in meetings				
complete tasks on time				
do my share of the work				
communicate effectively				
provide ideas				
participate and contribute				
support and encourage others				
express my feelings openly and appropriately				
constructively criticise				
be flexible and adaptable				
be confident				
enjoy it				

How could I have contributed more effectively?

4.3.3 Tutor-assessment of the support group process

You could arrange to observe the group during a group meeting and record the process according to pre-determined criteria. It is also possible to observe group and individual behaviour during a presentation.

Benefits

- **the tutor acts as an independent observer, to offer a more objective view**

- **students may see the tutor as offering specialist input to their group.**

Difficulties

- **time-consuming**

- **tutor may be seen as an intruder within the group - the members know they are being observed**

An example is given below:

Assignment Report - Front Sheet

Name of course member:		Year enrolled on Programme:	Centre:
Title of assignment:		Unit code:	Credit points:
Signature of tutor:	Academic level:	Recommendation to Assessment Board: **Pass / Fail**	
Submission date:	Date submitted to tutor:	Date returned by tutor:	

Your rating against the following criteria will provide you with feedback on the quality of your assignment. The criteria are not necessarily of equal importance and the comments relate to the academic level identified above.

Key:
3 = You have not met this criterion. You need to address this as a priority.
2 = You have met this criterion. However you need to consider how you will build on this/develop this further.
1 = You have met this criterion at a level which is appropriate for the stage of the programme.

Indicative criteria: General			
Evidence that the nature of the assignment has been negotiated with unit tutor	1	2	3
Evidence of self-assessment e.g. a self-assessment pro-forma completed	1	2	3
Assignment has a clear and appropriate title	1	2	3
Length of assignment relevant to unit size	1	2	3
Rationale for choice of assignment topic	1	2	3
Evidence of appropriate additional reading building on the taught element of unit	1	2	3
Appropriately referenced references included in a conventional, consistent and full bibliography	1	2	3
Use of non-discriminatory content, language and materials	1	2	3
Indicative criteria: Knowledge and understanding			
Assignment addresses areas relating to the learning outcomes of the unit	1	2	3
Understanding of relevant concepts, skills, terms. Where appropriate, these are defined/explained	1	2	3
Assignment shows reflection and/or analysis, building on descriptive elements	1	2	3
Indicative criteria: Presentation			
Ideas are organised and expressed clearly and concisely	1	2	3
Introduction provides a clear focus and signposts the objectives and structure of the assignment	1	2	3
Assignment shows logical development, structure and coherence	1	2	3
Appropriate/sensible conclusions reached	1	2	3

Assignment legible. Professional approach to the presentation of the assignment including at least one aspect of Information Technology	1	2	3
Where known, the use of IT from previous assignment is built upon	1	2	3
Appropriate standard of literacy and language e.g. spelling, grammar	1	2	3
Indicative criteria: Application to self and work situation			
Aspects of own practice/work situation linked to the ideas/arguments developed	1	2	3
Appropriate evidence of reflection and evaluation on practice as a teacher and learner. Implications for own work role and professional development explored	1	2	3

Assignment Report - Continuation Sheet

Name of course member: Unit Code:

Points for future consideration/action

Tutor comments

4.4 HOW WILL MARKS BE ALLOCATED?

More often than not, you are likely to be assessing a combination of academic understanding/knowledge, presentation, group process and individual skill development and so need to decide on a balance of mark allocation, for example:

- **60% for the product (individual/group report or presentation)**

- **20% for the group process**

- **20% for individual evaluation of development**

In some cases, you may be able to use the simpler pass/fail system.

4.4.1 Group marks

If the group is awarded a mark and all the members therefore gain the same mark, there may be an issue of inequality. There are advantages and disadvantages to any method of mark allocation for group work. It may be helpful to spend some time discussing this with students. You may want to consider how this can be done in the fairest way according to your particular aims, students and subject area. Some suggestions are listed below:

- **the mark is awarded and the students divide it up as they think appropriate e.g. a group of 5 students is given 15/20. The mark is multiplied by 5 (the number of people in the group) and the students share it out as they feel is appropriate. The two marks are then added together to give the final mark**

- **the tutor awards a group mark for the product. The students also award marks out of 10 for teamwork, contribution etc. The two marks are added together to give the final mark.**

- **a group product is given a group mark and each student also submits a mini-report on their particular task and their development. Both marks are added together.**

- **a learning contract clearly identifies each student's task. The group members identify criteria for each task and each student is assessed according to their own part of the contract.**

- **the group report is assessed, awarding a group mark and individual performances are assessed during the group presentation. The two marks are combined to provide an individual mark.**

An example is given on the next page:

Group-Assessment Sheet

Names of group members

Tutor's name

Date

Ratings: 4 = a major strength   2 = usually adequate
              3 = a strength   1 = a priority for development

✓

How the group worked	1	2	3	4	
meetings well organised					meetings were confusing
work shared evenly					uneven workload
all agreed decisions					decisions not made/not involve all
everyone did what they agreed					not everyone completed their work
used resources well					not use them well
achieved group goals					not achieved
used members abilities well					not used well
equal participation in discussions					some dominant or quiet members
listened and responded to others					ignored others or their ideas
helped each other					work uncooperatively
showed enthusiasm					showed apathy
express feelings openly					not express feelings
enjoyed working together					not enjoyed

How could the group have worked better?

4.4.2 Negotiating with students

Negotiating with students about how the marks could be allocated may encourage an element of student determination and help with the problems they feel over collective and individual responsibility. It will take time and skill on the tutor's part.

You may also feel you could negotiate all or some of the criteria for assessment to encourage ownership.

You could consider the following suggestions:

* **reaching a whole-group consensus, where all the students agree who will decide the mark allocation or the criteria**

* **allowing each group to decide on the allocation of all the marks or the criteria**

* **have a balance between student choice and tutor direction by allowing each group to determine how a portion of the marks is allocated or a selection of the criteria, while you determine the rest e.g. students use peer-assessment for assessing the oral presentation, each group determining or being given the criteria, while the tutor decides the mark for content**

* **each student could identify and negotiate their personal criteria for development**

4.5 WHAT EVIDENCE CAN BE PROVIDED?

Providing evidence to demonstrate how effectively the group functions or how an individual has developed is not easy.   The suggestions below provide some possible examples which students can collect and collate to demonstrate achievement of the assessment criteria.

Please tick those that interest you	
Minutes of meetings	☐
Structured sheets to complete. See p63	☐
Peer-assessment of how the members worked together. See p59	☐
An individual, critical comment on individual performance – self-assessment. See p61	☐
Logs or diaries	☐
Learning contract, indicating how far each criterion was met. See p26	☐
Portfolio of evidence of groupwork skills, to include some of the above	☐

4.5.1 Learning Contracts

A learning contract is an agreement made between the group members (see below and p26 for examples). It can be used to allocate tasks and indicate the timing of the project. Each student signs the contract. It can then be used to review individual roles in group work or as the basis for allocating marks – how far did each individual meet their targets?

Benefits

- **helps students plan tasks and timing**

- **develops negotiating skills**

- **clarifies responsibilities (and so helps with the problem of free-loaders)**

Difficulties

- **some students do not take them seriously – the tutor may need to emphasise the importance**

Learning Contract

Team members

1	3
2	4

Please discuss and agree, within your group and with your tutor, the tasks to be completed by each team member, under the following headings:

Report

Task relating to the report	To be done by whom?

Detailed plans

Task relating to the plans	To be done by whom?

Detailed constructional drawings

Task relating to the drawings	To be done by whom?

Verification of the learning contract: Students' signatures

1	3
2	4

Tutor signature   Date

4.5.2 Logs and diaries

Each group member writes an on-going record of what happened in the group, who contributed and what they did towards the task.

Benefits

* can aid reflection

* helps raise awareness of the group process

* helps raise awareness of their own development

Difficulties

* logs and diaries can be fabricated, even if each group member signs everyone's record

* students may not take them seriously unless assessed. (You could consider not assessing them directly, but stating that unless a log/diary of the group meetings is kept, no grade for the group assignment will be given).

4.5.3 Portfolios

Each student compiles a portfolio of evidence of the group process and the work carried out. This might, for example, include a diary, self-assessment exercises, the group report. At intervals during a programme/course, students could be given individual structured sheets, which focus on the group process and self-awareness, to complete during a group meeting. These could be added to a portfolio. It is important to be clear about what the portfolio is actually proving and how to make sure assessment criteria are appropriate.

Benefits

* flexible format is useful for students' personal and professional skill development

* helps develop reflective and analytical skills

* demonstrates the learning process

Difficulties

* can be time consuming to compile and assess

* students not knowing when to stop. Appropriateness of content to desired outcomes. There can be a tendency to put everything in

Portfolio Assessment Report

Name of Course Member: Cohort: Credit Points:

Signature of Tutor: Date: Pass/Fail

Your rating against the following criteria will provide you with some feedback on the quality of your portfolio. The comments relate to assessment at CATS level 1.

Learning Outcomes	Page		Achieved
• confidently use the course documentation	☐	—	☐
• know and understand the learning outcomes of the programme and how these will be achieved	☐	—	☐
• identify which study skills to develop to work confidently at level one	☐	—	☐
• use and apply references appropriate to developing your approach to learning related to your individual action plan	☐	—	☐
• effectively use the library and learning resources	☐	—	☐
• review your current approach to the planning and evaluation of your work load	☐	—	☐
• develop the knowledge of your subject area	☐	—	☐
• compare the approach used in your own institution with that of another institution	☐	—	☐
• develop your skills in self-reflection and action-planning	☐	—	☐
• recognise what support you need to develop your skills as an autonomous learner	☐	—	☐
• be more effective at working in a group	☐	—	☐
• recognise your strengths and interpersonal skills	☐	—	☐
• identify key issues in your own practice in relation to equal opportunities	☐	—	☐
• identify support for your professional development	☐	—	☐
• produce a contract negotiated with your mentor	☐	—	☐

4.5.4 Presentations

The group demonstrates what it has learnt by giving a presentation of the information e.g. timed oral presentation, poster, video, leaflet, role-play.

In a seminar, individual students could give a review of a book relating to the group task. This could count towards their individual assessment, to be combined with the group assessment.

An example is given below.

Oral Presentation Tutor and Peer Assessment

Name

Title of presentation

STRUCTURE					
introduction	good outline of purpose				unclear and confusing
	interesting and inviting				dry and dull
sequencing	logical				inconsistent, difficult to follow
	clear transition from one idea to another				muddled progression
conclusion	effective summary of key points				brief and unmemorable
	ends on a high note				is flat
CONTENT					
	well researched, evidence provided				poorly investigated
	main points clearly explained				long or confused explanations
DELIVERY					
voice	clear, well projected				muffled and quiet
	varies in tone and pace				monotonous
	uses inflection and pause for effect				speech is lifeless
body language	smiles, looks relaxed				appears uncomfortable
	uses eye contact				avoids contact
	confident manner and gestures				unhelpful mannerisms
visual aids	appropriate for the presentation				aids are irrelevant
	well prepared, clear and simple				difficult to read, wordy
	aids are presented effectively				hurried, not explained
audience	pitched appropriately for the audience				too high or too low level
	includes, involves audience				avoids audience
	clear and relevant replies to questions				muddled and confused
	audience interest maintained				audience bored
timing	keeps to time				runs over/under time

Comments

Tutor   date

4.5.5 Written assignments

Group report
The group members work together on the task and submit a joint report.

Individual report
Students work as a group to share the task of information-gathering, collating their material. Each student compiles her/his own report on the set task.

Essays
Essays are not commonly used as a method of group assessment, but could be used as a means of offering individual assessment combined with a group assessment.

SUMMARY

This chapter has covered the following:

- *Will you use assessment with support groups?*

- *What will you assess?*

- *Who will assess?*

- *How will you allocate marks?*

- *What evidence can be provided?*

You may wish to include elements of all or some of the suggestions in this chapter. It may be helpful to discuss with other unit tutors what and how they plan to assess, so that you are not duplicating effort and format.

Please consider the following in relation to your own teaching and learning situation. An example has been provided.

Task	Method of assessment	Weighting of mark	Who will assess?
Investigate the transport difficulties within Sheffield City Centre	Group presentation of results of investigation	40%	Tutor (20%) Peers (20%)
	Individual report	30%	Tutor (30%)
	Individual review of learning e.g. evidence of skill development in portfolio	30%	Tutor (20%) Student (10%)

5
DEALING WITH POTENTIAL DIFFICULTIES

5.1 What are the potential difficulties in using student support groups?
5.2 What are the strategies needed to overcome potential difficulties?
5.3 Summary

Working with support groups can bring many challenges, for both students and tutors. Some of the possible tensions within a group may well be part of the learning process itself (see Section 2.4.3) and can be important for the development of such skills as negotiating and communicating. The tutor's dilemma may be one of balance - when and how far to intervene to ensure the group's effectiveness.

This chapter will consider the following questions:

- **What are the potential difficulties in working with student support groups?**

- **What are the strategies needed to overcome potential difficulties?**

Successful student support group work may depend on a range of factors, from the learning context and the level of student skill, confidence, and experience, to tutor attitude and response. The majority of difficulties may be pre-empted by careful planning and monitoring.

5.1 WHAT ARE THE POTENTIAL DIFFICULTIES IN WORKING WITH STUDENT SUPPORT GROUPS?

Please tick those you have come across or would anticipate as the most likely.	
Difficulties with individual students	
A student is not attending classes or meetings	☐
A student is not doing what s/he says s/he will do	☐
A group member dominates the activities	☐
A student who disrupts the group by being negative	☐
A group member who does not contribute to discussions or offer ideas and information	☐
An individual does not see the value of the student group	☐
A student asks to move groups, for whatever reason	☐
A student is unhappy about the allocation of marks in the assessment	☐
A student is more geographically removed from other support group members	☐
Difficulties with the group	
The support group is not clear about the activity and/or aims	☐
The group does not see the value of support group work	☐
The group lacks motivation	☐
The group is disorganised/has no clear timetable/doesn't communicate effectively	☐
Group members are too geographically dispersed to meet	☐
The group wants to 'expel' a student	☐
The group would prefer to be set individual work carrying an individual mark	☐

5.2 WHAT ARE SOME OF THE STRATEGIES NEEDED TO OVERCOME POTENTIAL DIFFICULTIES?

5.2.1 Planning, monitoring and support

Although difficulties cannot be completely eliminated, their effects can be minimised through initial strategic planning, preparation and communication. You may recognise these strategies from working through the previous chapters:

- giving clear and unambiguous information - e.g. course and/or group structure, purpose, expectations/requirements, assessment and criteria. See Section 2. 3.1 (p 28)

- involving students in discussion and consultation by, for example, discussing possible difficulties which could arise and how they could be dealt with. This could help you identify possible support needs. See Section 2.2.1 (p25)

- giving consideration to the age, gender, background, confidence and experience of the students in your expectations. Certain students may need greater tutor support, for example.

- careful observation and monitoring of how the members of the support groups are working together. You could set aside a session for looking at issues of concern for students, either as a whole group, or in their support groups. It can help to agree clear boundaries.

- equipping students with essential skills for working in small groups. This could involve providing appropriate activities, for example, working through information and suggestions for working with others, dealing with people, problem solving etc.

- for distance learners - setting up clear structures for communication e.g. computer conferencing, residentials, contact with the tutor

- co-ordination with other courses/programmes e.g. do all the year's modules for example involve groupwork? Could there be some unifying sessions to introduce group work skills and raise student awareness? Are all the assessments to be in at the same time? Review meetings of staff and students would be useful: See Section 3.4 (p51)

- will all the tutors be giving the same information to the students and have similar expectations? Is there time set aside for tutors to meet and discuss issues arising during the course/programme?

- do you as a tutor need more information and support?

5.2.2 Encouraging the group to solve its own problems

This could be particularly relevant where the focus of a module, for example, is to develop skills. When a group clearly has difficulties and comes to you, the tutor, for help, the first approach is to establish the exact nature and history of the problem.

Please tick the questions you think it would be appropriate to ask and add your own below	
Have they asked the person who is not working/communicating why not? They may have good reason	☐
Have they written down and agreed what everyone is to do? Is there a Learning Contract? See example on p 26. Section 2.2.1	☐
Has the group made reasonable demands of each member? Is it an even work-load?	☐
Does each support group member understand their task/aims?	☐
Would it be appropriate to set agendas and take minutes of the meetings?	☐
Is the time set for support group meetings convenient for all?	☐
Are support group members clear about their goals?	☐
Are they being inclusive and fair?	☐
Has the support group taken account of individual circumstances/difficulties?	☐

You could invite the support group to draw up an Action Plan to try to address their difficulties. See below for an example:

Group Action Plan		
Name	Action and by when	Signed

5.2.3 Tutor intervention

The student support group may be unable to sort out their own difficulties and so may need support and guidance from you in resolving them. This will be more effectively dealt with through building support group tutorials into your programme. (See Section 3.2.1, p48) The following are some suggestions:

- **a support group tutorial could aim to discuss and resolve the problem, as a group. This could be done for dealing with difficulties of motivation, confusion over the task, problems in carrying out elements of the task etc. It could require confidence and counselling skills on your part, particularly where personality clashes are evident.**

- **invite the students to meet with you to draw up a new Learning Contract (see p 68). You could monitor progress.**

- **invite a non-participating support group member to an informal meeting to discuss the problems and negotiate solutions, re-examining the purpose of the support group work. It could be that referral to a Counselling Service may be appropriate when this may be caused by emotional stress, for example.**

- **write to the non-participating member to remind her/him of the course requirements (e.g. attendance, assessment).**

In some circumstances, tutors may need to take more action and make decisions, for example:

- **a non-productive student could be offered the opportunity to join another group, with its permission**

- **a non-productive group could be broken down to form two new groups, again, by negotiation and consultation**

- **non-participating students could be invited to work together, as a second chance**

- **if a student continues to be non-participating, it may be possible to ask her/him to do a piece of independent work, to be assessed by the same criteria as the groups. This could mean that any assessment marks for group work skills would not be awarded. Could the student still pass? See Chapter 4 on assessment.**

- **the student could be advised that he/she is likely to fail, (if the course requirements allow for this).**

You may find it helpful to discuss difficulties with other tutors, from either your own discipline or others, to explore possible options and strategies. At the end of this guide, there is a list of useful references.

SUMMARY

This chapter has covered the following areas:

- *Some of the potential difficulties in working with student support groups*

- *Strategies to help overcome the potential difficulties*

You might find it helpful to list the strategies you could adopt for the difficulties you identified at the beginning of this chapter

Strategies

6 CONCLUSION

Many more tutors are working with support groups, particularly with the move to develop more autonomous learning. Careful planning, preparation and monitoring will ensure the success of support groups and increase their long-term effectiveness.

How confident do you feel about working with support groups in the following areas? Please tick the appropriate column.

1. *Not clear - need more information/practice*
2. *Fairly confident*
3. *Very confident*

	1	2	3
Purpose/aims			
Your role			
Students' role			
Group structure			
Group management			
Structured support materials			
Assessment task(s)			
Assessment method			
Organisation of monitoring and support process e.g. attendance			
Organisation of interim reviews e.g. tutorials			
Organisation of final reviews			
Dealing with difficulties			

What do you see as the advantages of setting up and developing learner support groups for you and the students?	
You	**Students**

Are there any difficulties in setting up and developing learner support groups for you and the students?	
You	Students

You might find it useful to plan further action for the areas where you feel least confident. An Action Plan proforma is provided. It may be helpful to form your own support group with other staff working in this area.

Action Plan

Action needed	What could help?	Who could help?
Short term		
Medium term		
Long term		

7 REFERENCES

Aspinwall K, Simkins T, Wilkinson J F and Mc Auley J (1992) *Managing Evaluation in Education: A Development Approach,* London, Routledge

Boud, D (ed.) (1995) *Developing Student Autonomy in Learning, 2nd Edition,* London, Kogan Page

Brown, G (1993) 'Assessing student learning', ALTER Project, USDU Nottingham, University of Nottingham

Drew, S and Bingham, R (1997) *Student Skills Guide,* Aldershot, Gower

Earwaker, J (1992) *Helping and Supporting Students,* Buckingham, SRHE/Open University Press

Edwards, J (1991) *Evaluation in Adult and Further Education,* Liverpool, Workers' Educational Association

Finch, M and Daniels, J (1992) 'Tutor skills for open and flexible learning', unpublished

Gibbs, G (1992) *Independent Learning with More Students,* The Teaching More Students Project: PCFC, Oxford

Gibbs, G (1994) *Learning in Teams: A Student Manual,* Oxford Centre for Staff Development

Gibbs, G (1994) *Learning in Teams: A Student Guide,* Oxford Centre for Staff Development

Griffiths S, Partington P (1992) (Effective Learning and Technique in HE) *Module 5 Enabling Active Learning in Small Groups,* Sheffield, CVCP

Jaques, D (1989) *Independent Learning and Project Work,* Module 7, Certificate in Teaching in Higher Education by Open Learning, Oxford Centre for Staff Development

Lewis, R (1984) *How to Help Learners Assess their Progress,* London, Council for Education Technology

Lilley, A and Newton, S (1990) 'Mentorship: Supporting the adult learner. An investigation of the working of a mentorship scheme', *Journal of Further and Higher Education,* 14,3

Lindsey, R (1988) *Teaching Students to Help Themselves,* London, Kogan Page

Nelson-Jones, R (1988) *Practical Counselling and Helping Skills,* London, Cassell

Parsons, DE and Drew, SK, 'Designing group project work to enhance learning: key elements', *Teaching in Higher Education,* 1,1, 1996

Pettigrew M, and Elliott D, (forthcoming), *Student IT Skills,* Aldershot, Gower

Race, P (1986) *How to Win as an Open Learning Tutor,* London, Council for Educational Technology

Race, R (1989) *The Open Learning Handbook,* London, Kogan Page

Reynolds, M (1994) *Groupwork in Education and Training,* London, Kogan Page

Rowntree, D (1987) *Assessing Students: How Shall We Know Them?,* London, Kogan Page

Rowntree, D (1986) *Teaching Through Self-Instruction. How to Develop Open Learning Materials,* London, Kogan Page

Thornley, L and Gregory, R (eds) (1994) *Using Group Based Learning in Higher Education,* London, Kogan Page

Tuckman, B (1965) 'Developmental sequence in small groups', *Psychological Bulletin,* LXIII *(6)*

Tuckman, BW and Jensen, MAC (1977) 'Stages of small group development', *Group and Organisational Studies* 2, 4